This Journal belongs to

_____

Date..........................

Three things I'm grateful for today...

1._____

2._____

3._____

THANK YOU. THANK YOU. THANK YOU.

Something awesome
that happened to me today...

My level of happiness...

Date.........................

Three things I'm grateful for today...

1._____

2._____

3._____

THANK YOU. THANK YOU. THANK YOU.

Something awesome
that happened to me today...

My level of happiness...

Date.........................

Three things I'm grateful for today...

1._____

2._____

3._____

THANK YOU. THANK YOU. THANK YOU.

Something awesome
that happened to me today...

My level of happiness...

Date.........................

Three things I'm grateful for today...

1._____

2._____

3._____

THANK YOU. THANK YOU. THANK YOU.

Something awesome
that happened to me today...

My level of happiness...

Date..........................

Three things I'm grateful for today...

1._____

2._____

3._____

THANK YOU. THANK YOU. THANK YOU.

Something awesome
that happened to me today...

My level of happiness...

Date.........................

Three things I'm grateful for today...

1._____

2._____

3._____

THANK YOU. THANK YOU. THANK YOU.

Something awesome
that happened to me today...

My level of happiness...

Date.........................

Three things I'm grateful for today...

1._____

2._____

3._____

THANK YOU. THANK YOU. THANK YOU.

Something awesome
that happened to me today...

My level of happiness...

Date...........................

Three things I'm grateful for today...

1._____

2._____

3._____

THANK YOU. THANK YOU. THANK YOU.

Something awesome
that happened to me today...

My level of happiness...

Date.........................

Three things I'm grateful for today...

1._____

2._____

3._____

THANK YOU. THANK YOU. THANK YOU.

Something awesome
that happened to me today...

My level of happiness...

Date.........................

Three things I'm grateful for today...

1._____

2._____

3._____

THANK YOU. THANK YOU. THANK YOU.

Something awesome
that happened to me today...

My level of happiness...

Date.........................

Three things I'm grateful for today...

1._____

2._____

3._____

THANK YOU. THANK YOU. THANK YOU.

Something awesome
that happened to me today...

My level of happiness...

Date..........................

Three things I'm grateful for today...

1._____

2._____

3._____

THANK YOU. THANK YOU. THANK YOU.

Something awesome
that happened to me today...

My level of happiness...

Date..........................

Three things I'm grateful for today...

1._____

2._____

3._____

THANK YOU. THANK YOU. THANK YOU.

Something awesome
that happened to me today...

My level of happiness...

Date.........................

Three things I'm grateful for today...

1._____

2._____

3._____

THANK YOU. THANK YOU. THANK YOU.

Something awesome
that happened to me today...

My level of happiness...

Date..........................

Three things I'm grateful for today...

1._____

2._____

3._____

THANK YOU. THANK YOU. THANK YOU.

Something awesome
that happened to me today...

My level of happiness...

Date.........................

Three things I'm grateful for today...

1._____

2._____

3._____

THANK YOU. THANK YOU. THANK YOU.

Something awesome
that happened to me today...

My level of happiness...

Date..........................

Three things I'm grateful for today...

1._____

2._____

3._____

THANK YOU. THANK YOU. THANK YOU.

Something awesome
that happened to me today...

My level of happiness...

Date.........................

Three things I'm grateful for today...

1._____

2._____

3._____

THANK YOU. THANK YOU. THANK YOU.

Something awesome
that happened to me today...

My level of happiness...

Date.........................

Three things I'm grateful for today...

1._____

2._____

3._____

THANK YOU. THANK YOU. THANK YOU.

Something awesome
that happened to me today...

My level of happiness...

Date.........................

Three things I'm grateful for today...

1._____

2._____

3._____

THANK YOU. THANK YOU. THANK YOU.

Something awesome
that happened to me today...

My level of happiness...

Date..........................

Three things I'm grateful for today...

1._____

2._____

3._____

THANK YOU. THANK YOU. THANK YOU.

Something awesome
that happened to me today...

My level of happiness...

Date.........................

Three things I'm grateful for today...

1._____

2._____

3._____

THANK YOU. THANK YOU. THANK YOU.

Something awesome
that happened to me today...

My level of happiness...

Date.........................

Three things I'm grateful for today...

1._____

2._____

3._____

THANK YOU. THANK YOU. THANK YOU.

Something awesome
that happened to me today...

My level of happiness...

Date........................

Three things I'm grateful for today...

1._____

2._____

3._____

THANK YOU. THANK YOU. THANK YOU.

Something awesome
that happened to me today...

My level of happiness...

Date...........................

Three things I'm grateful for today...

1._____

2._____

3._____

THANK YOU. THANK YOU. THANK YOU.

Something awesome
that happened to me today...

My level of happiness...

Date.........................

Three things I'm grateful for today...

1._____

2._____

3._____

THANK YOU. THANK YOU. THANK YOU.

Something awesome
that happened to me today...

My level of happiness...

Date.........................

Three things I'm grateful for today...

1._____

2._____

3._____

THANK YOU. THANK YOU. THANK YOU.

Something awesome
that happened to me today...

My level of happiness...

Date..........................

Three things I'm grateful for today...

1._____

2._____

3._____

THANK YOU. THANK YOU. THANK YOU.

Something awesome
that happened to me today...

My level of happiness...

Date.........................

Three things I'm grateful for today...

1._____

2._____

3._____

THANK YOU. THANK YOU. THANK YOU.

Something awesome
that happened to me today...

My level of happiness...

Date.........................

Three things I'm grateful for today...

1._____

2._____

3._____

THANK YOU. THANK YOU. THANK YOU.

Something awesome
that happened to me today...

My level of happiness...

Date.........................

Three things I'm grateful for today...

1._____

2._____

3._____

THANK YOU. THANK YOU. THANK YOU.

Something awesome
that happened to me today...

My level of happiness...

Date..........................

Three things I'm grateful for today...

1._____

2._____

3._____

THANK YOU. THANK YOU. THANK YOU.

Something awesome
that happened to me today...

My level of happiness...

Date..........................

Three things I'm grateful for today...

1._____

2._____

3._____

THANK YOU. THANK YOU. THANK YOU.

Something awesome
that happened to me today...

My level of happiness...

Date.........................

Three things I'm grateful for today...

1._____

2._____

3._____

THANK YOU. THANK YOU. THANK YOU.

Something awesome
that happened to me today...

My level of happiness...

Date.........................

Three things I'm grateful for today...

1._____

2._____

3._____

THANK YOU. THANK YOU. THANK YOU.

Something awesome
that happened to me today...

My level of happiness...

Date.........................

Three things I'm grateful for today...

1._____

2._____

3._____

THANK YOU. THANK YOU. THANK YOU.

Something awesome
that happened to me today...

My level of happiness...

Date.........................

Three things I'm grateful for today...

1._____

2._____

3._____

THANK YOU. THANK YOU. THANK YOU.

Something awesome
that happened to me today...

My level of happiness...

Date..........................

Three things I'm grateful for today...

1._____

2._____

3._____

THANK YOU. THANK YOU. THANK YOU.

Something awesome
that happened to me today...

My level of happiness...

Date..........................

Three things I'm grateful for today...

1._____

2._____

3._____

THANK YOU. THANK YOU. THANK YOU.

Something awesome
that happened to me today...

My level of happiness...

Date..........................

Three things I'm grateful for today...

1._____

2._____

3._____

THANK YOU. THANK YOU. THANK YOU.

Something awesome
that happened to me today...

My level of happiness...

Date..........................

Three things I'm grateful for today...

1._____

2._____

3._____

THANK YOU. THANK YOU. THANK YOU.

Something awesome
that happened to me today...

My level of happiness...

Date..........................

Three things I'm grateful for today...

1._____

2._____

3._____

THANK YOU. THANK YOU. THANK YOU.

Something awesome
that happened to me today...

My level of happiness...

Date..........................

Three things I'm grateful for today...

1._____

2._____

3._____

THANK YOU. THANK YOU. THANK YOU.

Something awesome
that happened to me today...

My level of happiness...

Date...........................

Three things I'm grateful for today...

1._____

2._____

3._____

THANK YOU. THANK YOU. THANK YOU.

Something awesome
that happened to me today...

My level of happiness...

Date..........................

Three things I'm grateful for today...

1._____

2._____

3._____

THANK YOU. THANK YOU. THANK YOU.

Something awesome
that happened to me today...

My level of happiness...

Date.........................

Three things I'm grateful for today...

1._____

2._____

3._____

THANK YOU. THANK YOU. THANK YOU.

Something awesome
that happened to me today...

My level of happiness...

Date.........................

Three things I'm grateful for today...

1._____

2._____

3._____

THANK YOU. THANK YOU. THANK YOU.

Something awesome
that happened to me today...

My level of happiness...

Date.........................

Three things I'm grateful for today...

1._____

2._____

3._____

THANK YOU. THANK YOU. THANK YOU.

Something awesome
that happened to me today...

My level of happiness...

Date.........................

Three things I'm grateful for today...

1._____

2._____

3._____

THANK YOU. THANK YOU. THANK YOU.

Something awesome
that happened to me today...

My level of happiness...

Date.........................

Three things I'm grateful for today...

1._____

2._____

3._____

THANK YOU. THANK YOU. THANK YOU.

Something awesome
that happened to me today...

My level of happiness...

Date.........................

Three things I'm grateful for today...

1._____

2._____

3._____

THANK YOU. THANK YOU. THANK YOU.

Something awesome
that happened to me today...

My level of happiness...

Date.........................

Three things I'm grateful for today...

1._____

2._____

3._____

THANK YOU. THANK YOU. THANK YOU.

Something awesome
that happened to me today...

My level of happiness...

Date............................

Three things I'm grateful for today...

1._____

2._____

3._____

THANK YOU. THANK YOU. THANK YOU.

Something awesome
that happened to me today...

My level of happiness...

Date...........................

Three things I'm grateful for today...

1._____

2._____

3._____

THANK YOU. THANK YOU. THANK YOU.

Something awesome
that happened to me today...

My level of happiness...

Date..........................

Three things I'm grateful for today...

1._____

2._____

3._____

THANK YOU. THANK YOU. THANK YOU.

Something awesome
that happened to me today...

My level of happiness...

Date.........................

Three things I'm grateful for today...

1._____

2._____

3._____

THANK YOU. THANK YOU. THANK YOU.

Something awesome
that happened to me today...

My level of happiness...

Date..........................

Three things I'm grateful for today...

1._____

2._____

3._____

THANK YOU. THANK YOU. THANK YOU.

Something awesome
that happened to me today...

My level of happiness...

Date.........................

Three things I'm grateful for today...

1._____

2._____

3._____

THANK YOU. THANK YOU. THANK YOU.

Something awesome
that happened to me today...

My level of happiness...

Date.........................

Three things I'm grateful for today...

1._____

2._____

3._____

THANK YOU. THANK YOU. THANK YOU.

Something awesome
that happened to me today...

My level of happiness...

Date..........................

Three things I'm grateful for today...

1._____

2._____

3._____

THANK YOU. THANK YOU. THANK YOU.

Something awesome
that happened to me today...

My level of happiness...

Date..........................

Three things I'm grateful for today...

1._____

2._____

3._____

THANK YOU. THANK YOU. THANK YOU.

Something awesome
that happened to me today...

My level of happiness...

Date.........................

Three things I'm grateful for today...

1._____

2._____

3._____

THANK YOU. THANK YOU. THANK YOU.

Something awesome
that happened to me today...

My level of happiness...

Date.........................

Three things I'm grateful for today...

1._____

2._____

3._____

THANK YOU. THANK YOU. THANK YOU.

Something awesome
that happened to me today...

My level of happiness...

Three things I'm grateful for today...

1._____

2._____

3._____

THANK YOU. THANK YOU. THANK YOU.

Something awesome
that happened to me today...

My level of happiness...

Date..........................

Three things I'm grateful for today...

1._____

2._____

3._____

THANK YOU. THANK YOU. THANK YOU.

Something awesome
that happened to me today...

My level of happiness...

Date.........................

Three things I'm grateful for today...

1._____

2._____

3._____

THANK YOU. THANK YOU. THANK YOU.

Something awesome
that happened to me today...

My level of happiness...

Date.........................

Three things I'm grateful for today...

1._____

2._____

3._____

THANK YOU. THANK YOU. THANK YOU.

Something awesome
that happened to me today...

My level of happiness...

Date.........................

Three things I'm grateful for today...

1._____

2._____

3._____

THANK YOU. THANK YOU. THANK YOU.

Something awesome
that happened to me today...

My level of happiness...

Date..........................

Three things I'm grateful for today...

1._____

2._____

3._____

THANK YOU. THANK YOU. THANK YOU.

Something awesome
that happened to me today...

My level of happiness...

Date........................

Three things I'm grateful for today...

1._____

2._____

3._____

THANK YOU. THANK YOU. THANK YOU.

Something awesome
that happened to me today...

My level of happiness...

Date........................

Three things I'm grateful for today...

1._____

2._____

3._____

THANK YOU. THANK YOU. THANK YOU.

Something awesome
that happened to me today...

My level of happiness...

Date.........................

Three things I'm grateful for today...

1._____

2._____

3._____

THANK YOU. THANK YOU. THANK YOU.

Something awesome
that happened to me today...

My level of happiness...

Date.........................

Three things I'm grateful for today...

1._____

2._____

3._____

THANK YOU. THANK YOU. THANK YOU.

Something awesome
that happened to me today...

My level of happiness...

Date.........................

Three things I'm grateful for today...

1._____

2._____

3._____

THANK YOU. THANK YOU. THANK YOU.

Something awesome
that happened to me today...

My level of happiness...

Date..........................

Three things I'm grateful for today...

1._____

2._____

3._____

THANK YOU. THANK YOU. THANK YOU.

Something awesome
that happened to me today...

My level of happiness...

Date.........................

Three things I'm grateful for today...

1._____

2._____

3._____

THANK YOU. THANK YOU. THANK YOU.

Something awesome
that happened to me today...

My level of happiness...

Date..........................

Three things I'm grateful for today...

1._____

2._____

3._____

THANK YOU. THANK YOU. THANK YOU.

Something awesome
that happened to me today...

My level of happiness...

Date.........................

Three things I'm grateful for today...

1._____

2._____

3._____

THANK YOU. THANK YOU. THANK YOU.

Something awesome
that happened to me today...

My level of happiness...

Date..........................

Three things I'm grateful for today...

1._____

2._____

3._____

THANK YOU. THANK YOU. THANK YOU.

Something awesome
that happened to me today...

My level of happiness...

Date..........................

Three things I'm grateful for today...

1._____

2._____

3._____

THANK YOU. THANK YOU. THANK YOU.

Something awesome
that happened to me today...

My level of happiness...

Date.........................

Three things I'm grateful for today...

1._____

2._____

3._____

THANK YOU. THANK YOU. THANK YOU.

Something awesome
that happened to me today...

My level of happiness...

Date.........................

Three things I'm grateful for today...

1._____

2._____

3._____

THANK YOU. THANK YOU. THANK YOU.

Something awesome
that happened to me today...

My level of happiness...

Date..........................

Three things I'm grateful for today...

1._____

2._____

3._____

THANK YOU. THANK YOU. THANK YOU.

Something awesome
that happened to me today...

My level of happiness...

Date..........................

Three things I'm grateful for today...

1._____

2._____

3._____

THANK YOU. THANK YOU. THANK YOU.

Something awesome
that happened to me today...

My level of happiness...

Date..........................

Three things I'm grateful for today...

1._____

2._____

3._____

THANK YOU. THANK YOU. THANK YOU.

Something awesome
that happened to me today...

My level of happiness...

Date..........................

Three things I'm grateful for today...

1._____

2._____

3._____

THANK YOU. THANK YOU. THANK YOU.

Something awesome
that happened to me today...

My level of happiness...

Date..........................

Three things I'm grateful for today...

1._____

2._____

3._____

THANK YOU. THANK YOU. THANK YOU.

Something awesome
that happened to me today...

My level of happiness...

Date.........................

Three things I'm grateful for today...

1._____

2._____

3._____

THANK YOU. THANK YOU. THANK YOU.

Something awesome
that happened to me today...

My level of happiness...

Date...........................

Three things I'm grateful for today...

1._____

2._____

3._____

THANK YOU. THANK YOU. THANK YOU.

Something awesome
that happened to me today...

My level of happiness...

Date..........................

Three things I'm grateful for today...

1._____

2._____

3._____

THANK YOU. THANK YOU. THANK YOU.

Something awesome
that happened to me today...

My level of happiness...

Date.........................

Three things I'm grateful for today...

1._____

2._____

3._____

THANK YOU. THANK YOU. THANK YOU.

Something awesome
that happened to me today...

My level of happiness...

Date.........................

Three things I'm grateful for today...

1._____

2._____

3._____

THANK YOU. THANK YOU. THANK YOU.

Something awesome
that happened to me today...

My level of happiness...

Date........................

Three things I'm grateful for today...

1._____

2._____

3._____

THANK YOU. THANK YOU. THANK YOU.

Something awesome
that happened to me today...

My level of happiness...

Date.........................

Three things I'm grateful for today...

1._____

2._____

3._____

THANK YOU. THANK YOU. THANK YOU.

Something awesome
that happened to me today...

My level of happiness...

Date..........................

Three things I'm grateful for today...

1._____

2._____

3._____

THANK YOU. THANK YOU. THANK YOU.

Something awesome
that happened to me today...

My level of happiness...

Date.........................

Three things I'm grateful for today...

1._____

2._____

3._____

THANK YOU. THANK YOU. THANK YOU.

Something awesome
that happened to me today...

My level of happiness...

Date.........................

Three things I'm grateful for today...

1._____

2._____

3._____

THANK YOU. THANK YOU. THANK YOU.

Something awesome
that happened to me today...

My level of happiness...

Date..........................

Three things I'm grateful for today...

1._____

2._____

3._____

THANK YOU. THANK YOU. THANK YOU.

Something awesome
that happened to me today...

My level of happiness...

Date...........................

Three things I'm grateful for today...

1._____

2._____

3._____

THANK YOU. THANK YOU. THANK YOU.

Something awesome
that happened to me today...

My level of happiness...

Date........................

Three things I'm grateful for today...

1._____

2._____

3._____

THANK YOU. THANK YOU. THANK YOU.

Something awesome
that happened to me today...

My level of happiness...

Made in the USA
Las Vegas, NV
10 February 2024

85583865R00057